Actively promoting British values in the EYFS

Planning activities that foster core British values in your setting

by Marianne Sargent

Contents

Published by Practical Pre-School Books, A Division of MA Education Ltd, St Jude's Church, Dulwich Road, Herne Hill, London, SE24 0PB.

Tel: 020 7738 5454 www.practicalpreschoolbooks.com

© MA Education Ltd 2016

Design: Alison Coombes **fonthillcreative** 01722 717043

All images © MA Education with the excpetion of page 7 © iStockphoto.com/&#169 ariadna de Raadt; page 10 © iStockphoto.com/SerrNovik; page 11 © AdobeStock/annanahabed; page 13 © iStockphoto.com/Catherine Lane; page 14 © AdobeStock/Daddy Cool; page 19 © iStockphoto.com/Rakdee; page 20 © iStockphoto.com/pelvidge.

ISBN 978-1-909280-96-0

Introduction

What are 'British values'?

The Prevent aspect of the UK Government's counter-terrorism strategy places a duty on 'specified authorities' in England, Scotland and Wales, including schools, nurseries, pre-schools, childminders and day care providers, to 'ensure that [children] are taught in a way that is consistent with the law and our values'. The Government contends that 'terrorism is associated with rejection of a cohesive, integrated, multifaith society and of parliamentary democracy' and suggests prevention of radicalisation is 'dependent on developing a sense of belonging to this country and a support for our core values'. It refers to these as 'fundamental British values' and defines them as:

- Democracy

- The rule of law

- Individual liberty

- Mutual respect and tolerance of different faiths and beliefs.

(Prevent Strategy, HM Government, 2011)

The use of the term 'British values' and the values identified have been subject to contentious debate. This is touched on and briefly discussed in the companion to this book, *Promoting Fundamental British Values in the Early Years*. However, for the purpose of each publication and to avoid confusion the term 'British values' is maintained and used throughout both.

Democracy

The fundamental principle of democracy is 'rule by the people'. The ideals of democracy promote a shared belief in fairness and equality and a right to participate in important decision making. Arising from these ideals is an emphasis on shared responsibility, mutual respect and the wider community.

Rule of law

The rule of law is underpinned by an understanding that a democratic society can only succeed if citizens abide by the rules. People who live in a law-abiding society are able to distinguish right from wrong and understand the consequences of their actions in terms of how they impact upon other individuals and society as a whole.

Individual liberty

This is the personal freedom to make choices, voice opinions and portray an individual identity without fear of oppression, discrimination or censure. In order to exercise individual liberty people need self-belief and self-awareness because not only does this give them the self-confidence to express themselves, it also helps to prevent them looking outwards and hurting others.

Mutual respect and tolerance

The expectation that people of different races, with different faiths, from varying cultural backgrounds and with opposing views and beliefs should be able to live and work together in peace. A respectful and tolerant society accepts and respects difference, and appreciates the value of diversity and the rich opportunities it presents.

British values and the EYFS

'Early years providers already focus on children's personal, social and emotional development. The Early Years Foundation Stage framework supports early years providers to do this in an age appropriate way, through ensuring children learn right from wrong, mix and share with other children and value others' views, know about similarities and differences between themselves and others, and challenge negative attitudes and stereotypes.'

(Revised Prevent Duty Guidance for England and Wales, HM Government, 2015).

The values of democracy, rule of law, individual liberty, and mutual respect and tolerance of different faiths and beliefs are implicit within the themes and principles of the Statutory Framework for the Early Years Foundation Stage (EYFS). The underlying principle of 'A unique child' is that individual children should be respected and have access to early years provision that fosters their unique aptitudes and abilities, enabling them to thrive and develop. Through positive relationships children develop personal confidence and learn to become more independent. They develop a sense of right and wrong and learn how to regulate their own behaviour. Practitioners plan to provide enabling environments where children feel secure and able to take risks with their learning, encouraging them to become creative and critical thinkers.

The EYFS is a democratic curriculum that acknowledges the difference in the learning and development of individual children. Observation is central to early years practice and is used to inform planning so that provision meets the needs and interests of individual children. The EYFS gives children the freedom to play, explore and learn in their own way and encourages them to find out for themselves. It aims to motivate children to have a go, persist in their efforts and celebrate their achievements, as well as to manage their feelings and behaviour when things do not turn out as planned. What's more, it encourages children to have their own ideas, make their own choices and express their own opinions.

How to use this book

This is a practical resource that takes each of the British values in turn and demonstrates how they can be actively promoted in the early years setting. To begin with, page 4 takes a closer look at each of the four values and outlines the skills, aptitudes, abilities and attitudes that underpin them, highlighting what children need to learn, develop and understand in order to uphold them.

Pages 6 to 21 contain a range of activity ideas that aim to help children develop each of these underpinning skills, aptitudes and abilities. There are four activities for each British value. Each is described in detail with discussion ideas, as well as a list of resources, suggested key questions and curriculum links. On page 5 there is a planning matrix which provides an overview of these activities, the values they promote and how they link to the EYFS curriculum.

The end of the book looks at meeting the requirements of the Common Inspection Framework with ideas for how to collect

evidence that the setting is actively promoting British values. There is a brief checklist to help practitioners consider how settings can embed British values into everyday practice. Furthermore, there is an example observation document that can be used alongside the activities in the book with helpful prompts to aid assessment and reflection. Finally, there are suggestions for resources and further reading.

Actively promoting British values

Democracy, rule of law, individual liberty, and mutual respect and tolerance of different faiths and beliefs should be embedded in a setting's culture through everyday practice. Children look to adults for example and so these values should be promoted through the ethos of the setting and reflected in its policies and procedures.

The values cannot be taught. As a colleague put it: 'British values are exemplified rather than described. They are organic and moving and children are better served learning about why we have particular laws and what they are intended to protect'. The aim is not to tell children how to behave and what to think, it is to give them the knowledge and skills they need to regulate their own behaviour and make carefully considered, informed decisions. This equates with the characteristics of effective learning identified in the EYFS. Children must be engaged, motivated and encouraged to think for themselves.

While the companion to this book, *Promoting Fundamental British Values in the Early Years*, takes an in-depth look at each of the values in relation to the principles that underpin them, *Actively promoting British values in the EYFS* provides

Individual liberty

In order to enjoy individual liberty children need to have a sense of self and positive self-esteem so they have the self-confidence to portray a personal identity, express personal views and exercise freedom of choice. They also need to have the communication and language skills to convey their ideas and opinions, as well as listen to the views of others. It is important that we enable children to exercise their rights to personal freedoms from the earliest age, and encourage them to respect the freedom of others.

Mutual respect and tolerance

In order to promote mutual respect and tolerance we need to create an inclusive learning environment where all children and their families feel welcome and comfortable and negative and discriminatory attitudes are challenged. Children should learn about a variety of cultures and traditions in order that they can develop an understanding of different faiths and beliefs. They should explore similarities and differences between themselves and others so they grow up understanding, valuing and appreciating difference.

ideas for activities that reflect the characteristics of effective learning and aim to help children develop the knowledge, understanding, skills, aptitudes, abilities and attitudes that they need to uphold each of the values.

Democracy

The success of a democracy is reliant upon active participation. We should, therefore, encourage young children to get actively involved by asking them to share their ideas and opinions and inviting them to participate in decision-making processes. One of the ideals that underpins democracy is fair and equal treatment. In the early years this means learning to share, take turns and play cooperatively. Furthermore, a democratic society takes shared responsibility. As future participants in this democracy children need to learn to respect each other and work together.

Rule of law

In order to ensure children grow up with respect for the rule of law they need to be able to distinguish right from wrong and develop an understanding of the consequences of their actions. This means helping children to become emotionally literate so they are able to recognise different feelings and understand how emotions affect behaviour. It also means teaching them how to manage such feelings, regulate their behaviour and take responsibility. However, this does not mean raising children to blindly follow rules and regulations. They should be allowed to question authority and invited to engage in debate. To follow the rule of law children need to be able to pay attention, listen and process instructions and rules.

Planning matrix

Democracy	Rule of law	Individual liberty	Mutual respect and tolerance
Activity 1: Giant jigsaw **Key learning:** Sharing, participating, working together and cooperating **EYFS curriculum links:** PSED, CL, PD	**Activity 1:** On the road **Key learning:** Understanding need for rules, taking responsibility, considering consequences **EYFS curriculum links:** PSED, CL, PD, L, UW, EAD	**Activity 1:** We've all got talent! **Key learning:** Developing self-confidence and communication skills **EYFS curriculum links:** PSED, CL, EAD	**Activity 1:** Story wall **Key learning:** Learning about and understanding different faiths and beliefs **EYFS curriculum links:** CL, PD, L, UW, EAD
Activity 2: Catch the dragon's tail **Key learning:** Working together and cooperating **EYFS curriculum links:** PSED, CL, PD	**Activity 2:** Scribbling feelings **Key learning:** Recognising, understanding and describing emotions **EYFS curriculum links:** PSED, CL, PD, EAD	**Activity 2:** A problem shared **Key learning:** Communicating ideas and opinions, and listening to, accepting and respecting the views of others **EYFS curriculum links:** PSED, CL, UW	**Activity 2:** Symbolic art **Key learning:** Learning that British society is composed of many different faiths and beliefs **EYFS curriculum links:** PSED, PD, UW, EAD
Activity 3: Taking ownership **Key learning:** Participating, sharing ideas, developing respect for each other and working together **EYFS curriculum links:** PSED, CL, EAD	**Activity 3:** Dilemma! **Key learning:** Distinguishing between right and wrong, questioning authority, engaging in debate **EYFS curriculum links:** PSED, CL	**Activity 3:** Provoking a reaction **Key learning:** Communicating ideas and opinions, listening to the views of others, exercising right to individual creative thought and expression **EYFS curriculum links:** PSED, CL, UW, EAD	**Activity 3:** Same difference **Key learning:** Learning about and understanding different faiths and beliefs **EYFS curriculum links:** PSED, CL, UW
Activity 4: Safe passage **Key learning:** Participating, sharing ideas, cooperating, working together **EYFS curriculum links:** PSED, CL, PD	**Activity 4:** Beanbag catch **Key learning:** Paying attention, listening, processing, following rules **EYFS curriculum links:** PSED, CL, PD	**Activity 4:** Natural creations **Key learning:** Exercising right to individual creative expression **EYFS curriculum links:** PSED, CL, PD, UW, EAD	**Activity 4:** Flying visit **Key learning:** Learning about and understanding different countries and cultures **EYFS curriculum links:** PSED, UW, EAD

Democracy

Activity 1

Giant jigsaw

Resources

Giant 3D puzzles
Large wooden blocks or crates
Large cardboard boxes, junk and craft materials

What you do

It is easiest to do this activity with small groups of four or five children. However, the more children there are, the more they will be required to cooperate, share and compromise.

Challenge the children to work together to build a large 3D puzzle. If you do not have any large 3D puzzles, challenge them to build a castle/pirate ship using large wooden blocks or crates, or to make a big bus/space ship out of big cardboard boxes and junk. Any such collaborative activity will have the same learning outcomes.

Practise democratic decision making by asking the children to vote on which puzzle they would like to build or which model they would like to make. Ask for a show of hands, count how many vote for each option and mark the results on a whiteboard with tally marks. Point out which option has the largest number of votes and explain this is the majority vote because it is the most popular.

Remain with the group as they build the chosen puzzle/model, ensuring everyone gets to take an active role in the process. If they are building a relatively simple puzzle, ensure they take turns adding the pieces. If they are developing an intricate model, ensure they listen to each other's ideas and try out each other's suggestions. If need be, mediate when they disagree or argue about the task.

How does this promote democracy?

The ideals of democracy promote fairness, equality and active participation in decision-making. The initial vote to decide which puzzle/model to build is an example of democratic decision making. The group work that follows fosters collaboration and team work. The children are required to listen to each other's ideas and cooperate with each other.

Key questions/prompts

- Is everyone working together?

- How are you ensuring no-one is left out?
- Are you listening to each other?
- Tell me about your idea.
- Why don't you agree?
- What might happen if…?
- How do you know that will work?
- Have you tried…?
- Whose turn is it?

Curriculum links

PSED: Plays cooperatively, taking turns with others; takes account of one another's ideas about how to organise their activity; confident to speak in a familiar group and will talk about their ideas; beginning to be able to negotiate and solve problems without aggression.
CL: Gives their attention to what others say and responds appropriately; expresses themselves effectively, showing awareness of listeners' needs; uses talk to organise, sequence and clarify thinking and ideas.
PD: Handles construction materials safely and with increasing control.

Activity 2   Catch the dragon's tail

Resources

Wide open space
Dragon mask

What you do

Play this traditional game in a large open space, preferably outside on the grass. The game is more effective if played with a large number of children, however it is possible to play it with as few as 10. Ask the children to form a line and place their hands on the shoulders of the child in front. The child at the front end of the line is the dragon's head (and can wear a dragon mask) and the child at the back end is the tip of its tail.

The object of the game is for the head to catch the tail. The tail must try to avoid being caught. The children must not let their hands slip off the shoulders of the child in front and the line must not break up. This means the children have to work together to ensure they remain linked and do not fall over, while moving in tandem with each other to move the head toward the tail and the tail away from the head. Once the head manages to catch the tail, the child at the tip of the tail joins the front of the line to become the head and the game starts again.

As the children play this game step back and give them the space to try and work out a strategy for themselves. Encourage them to talk to and help each other. If they are struggling somewhat intervene and ask them to think about why they are having trouble succeeding.

Play other games that require team work and cooperation, for example, capture the flag, dodgeball, relay racing and all kinds of parachute activities.

How does this promote democracy?

Two of the underlying principles of democracy are shared responsibility and active participation. Team games help young children understand the power of collaboration and cooperation as they work together to achieve a common goal.

Key questions

- Are you working together?
- How do you think that happened?
- What might you try this time?

- Is it safe to play the game like that?
- Does anyone have another idea?
- What might happen if…?
- Can you remember the rules?
- Was that fair?

Curriculum links

PSED: Plays co-operatively; takes account of one another's ideas about how to organise their activity; confident to speak in a familiar group and will talk about their ideas; works as part of a group or class, and understands and follows the rules.
CL: Listens attentively in a range of situations; follows instructions involving several ideas or actions; expresses themselves effectively, showing awareness of the listeners' needs.
PD: Shows good control and co-ordination in large movements; moves confidently in a range of ways, safely negotiating space.

Democracy

Activity 3

Taking ownership

What you do

Every few weeks bring the children together and ask them what themes they would like for the role play area. List their suggestions on a large whiteboard and explain you will take a vote to see which are the most popular suggestions. Tell the children they can vote as many times as they like. Count the votes and mark them as tally marks against each option. The three options with the highest number of votes will be the role play themes for the next three weeks.

Then, at the end of the week bring the children together again. Remind them what the role play theme for the following week will be and ask them what they will need to create it. Compile a list of ideas for scenery, props, costumes and other resources. Ask the children to bring in anything they might want to use from home and gather everything you need over the weekend.

Set up the role play area each Monday morning and invite the children to help. Ask them to suggest how you should organise the space and where different props should be placed. Encourage them to use their imaginations and help create a backdrop and scenery.

As the children play in the area ask them if there is anything else it could benefit from. Is there anything missing? How might it be improved. Then at the end of each day encourage the children to take responsibility for tidying the area.

- Which is the most popular?
- How many votes did this theme get?
- What do you think we will need to set this up?
- Where do you think I can get that from?
- Do you think this works?
- Have we forgotten anything?
- Is there anything else you need/want?
- How can we make it better?

How does this promote democracy?

Involving children in planning and setting up the role play area is democratic practice because it ensures their active participation in creating their own play space. The role play area is a significant part of the early years setting and it makes sense to ensure the changing themes reflect the interests of the children. Demonstrate democracy in action by holding a vote to decide on the most popular themes and encouraging children to work together to make their ideas a reality.

Key questions

- What is your favourite role play theme?

Curriculum links

PSED: Takes account of one another's ideas about how to organise their activity; confident to speak to others about own needs, wants, interests and opinions.
CL: Uses talk to organise, sequence and clarify thinking and ideas.
EAD: Plays cooperatively as part of a group to develop and act out a narrative; represents their own ideas, thoughts and feelings through role play and stories.

Democracy

Activity 4

Safe passage

Resources

Toy alien
Role play space suits
Drapes
Cardboard boxes
Craft materials
Skipping ropes
Buckets
Netting
Blankets
Broom handle

What you do

Use the drapes, cardboard boxes and craft materials to create an otherworldly role play area somewhere in the setting (outside where there is more space is best). Then place a toy alien in a precarious position of peril, making sure it is well out of reach. It might be high up on a 'rocky ledge' or in a 'swamp', for instance.

Build a makeshift space buggy out of another large cardboard box and put some props in the back such as space suits, skipping ropes, netting, buckets, blankets and a broom handle.

Explain to the children they have been sent out on a rescue mission to a strange planet to find and rescue a missing alien. The only equipment they have is in the back of the space buggy and they must work together to figure out how they can use the equipment to bring the alien back to safety. It may be necessary to use your imagination to embellish the story slightly to increase the challenge. For example, if it is in a swamp you could suggest that the swamp is very deep and full of monsters so the children cannot set foot in it, meaning they must find a way to rescue the alien from the swamp edge. Or, if it is up in a tree or on a high wall and can be reached with the aid of a chair, perhaps suggest the ground is too unstable for chairs and ladders so the children must do without.

How does this promote democracy?

Like in Activity 2, this problem-solving task requires the children to take on shared responsibility, get actively involved and work as a team. As well as physically working together to reach the alien, they also need to talk to each other and work out a strategy. It is another way to demonstrate the power of collaboration and cooperation as the children work together to achieve a common goal.

Key questions

- What do you think you need to do?
- Do you have any ideas about how to solve this problem?
- What might happen if…?
- Why didn't that work?
- What do you think you could do instead?
- Is that safe?
- How do you think you could use that?

Curriculum links

PSED: Takes account of one another's ideas about how to organise their activity; confident to speak in a familiar group, will talk about their ideas, and will choose the resources they need; says when they do or don't need help.
CL: Listens and responds to ideas expressed by others in conversation or discussion; uses talk to organise, sequence and clarify thinking and ideas.
PD: Shows good control and co-ordination in large and small movements; handles equipment and tools effectively.
MD: Uses everyday language to talk about size, weight, capacity, position and distance.
EAD: Plays cooperatively as part of a group to develop and act out a narrative.

Rule of Law

Activity 1

On the road

What you do

Begin by sharing a book about road safety with the children. Surprisingly there are not many to choose from. However, *Watch Out! On the Road* by Claire Llewellyn and Mike Gordon covers a range of safety issues for children as pedestrians, car passengers, cyclists and users of public transport.

Use the book to raise discussion about the need for rules on the road and traffic laws. Find out how much the children know about road safety law. Can they explain the reason for different laws? Look at some road signs and talk about what they mean. Look at signs that set out rules such as speed limits, one way traffic, no stopping and no entry, and other signs that advise of hazards like roadworks or people/animals crossing. In addition, talk about road markings and what they mean, as well as the lights on crossings and what the different colours signal.

Set up a role-play roadway in the outdoor area. Use playground chalks to mark out a network of roads. Either create a one-way system or two-way streets. Mark out zebra and pelican crossings and put yellow lines in places where it is unsafe to park. Write the word SLOW near bends in the roads and set up some roadworks. As the children ride their play vehicles on the roads point out give way and stop signs. Explain the difference between using zebra and pelican crossings. Ask them to consider what would happen if they broke any of the rules of the road. What might the consequences be if a vehicle ignored a red light at some roadworks, for example? If you do not have these large-scale resources set up a small world roadway instead.

How does this promote the rule of law?

Road safety is ideal for exploring the need for laws and rules because it is something the children can easily relate to. The consequences of disregarding the rules of the road can be extremely serious so this is a helpful analogy for helping

children to make links between behaviour, choices, possible repercussions and taking responsibility.

Key questions

- Why do you think we need rules and laws for the roads?
- How do we know what the rules on the roads are?
- What might happen if we ignore road signs or break the rules of the road?
- Why is it important to do what road signs tell us?
- Have you ever been involved in a road accident? What happened? Why?

Curriculum links

PSED: Talks about their own and others' behaviour and its consequences, and knows that some behaviour is unacceptable.
CL: Answers 'how' and 'why' questions about their experiences and in response to stories or events.
PD: Shows understanding of the need for safety; talks about ways to keep safe.
L: Recognises familiar words and signs; knows that print carries meaning.
UW: Talks about why things happen and how things work.
EAD: Represents their own ideas and thoughts through role-play and stories.

Activity 2

Scribbling feelings

Resources

Multicoloured playground chalks
Mixing pallets and water
Powder paints
Paintbrushes
Laminated pictures of faces depicting a range of feelings
Access to a range of natural objects and materials

What you do

Explain you would like the children to use playground chalks to create pictures that portray different feelings. Begin by talking about different emotions and how they make us feel. Initially, it is best to concentrate on the basics, feelings that all children will easily understand and relate to, for example, anger, happiness, sadness and fear. Talk about each feeling in turn, asking the children to describe them as best they can. Are they able to tell you about a time when they were particularly angry, happy, sad or scared?

Go outside to an open space and ask them to think about how different feelings might make them want to move. Demonstrate stamping your feet in anger, jumping up and down for joy, lying down in despair and cowering with fear. Can the children think of any other movements?

Take a look at the different coloured chalks and ask the children which colours they think match each of the feelings best. Divide the children into groups and explain you would like each group to create a picture of a feeling. Allow the children to choose which emotion they would like to draw then stand back and give them space to get creative. Provide powder paints and encourage the children to incorporate natural objects into their pictures as well. Reassure them that their pictures do not have to be anything in particular, they can just be forms, shapes and colours.

When the pictures are complete, bring the children together to look at what they have created. Encourage children from each group to talk about their drawings and how/why they represent a particular feeling.

How does this promote the rule of law?

The aim of this activity is to help children explore the feelings engendered by different emotions in order to help them gain an understanding of the correlation between feelings and behaviour. Children who have a greater understanding of their emotions will be better able to regulate their behaviour and

exercise self-control. They will also find it easier to empathise with and comprehend the actions of others.

Key questions

- What does anger/happiness/sadness/fear make you feel like?
- What do you want to do when you are feeling angry/happy/sad/scared?
- Where do you want to go when you are feeling angry/happy/sad/scared?
- What colour/shape do you think anger/happiness/sadness/fear is?
- Is there anything else you could add?
- Why does that remind you of anger/happiness/sadness/fear?

Curriculum links

PSED: Talks about how they and others show feelings.
CL: Uses talk to organise, sequence and clarify thinking, ideas and feelings.
PD: Holds chalk/brush near point between first two fingers and thumb and uses it with good control.
EAD: Represents their own ideas, thoughts and feelings through art.

Rule of Law

Activity 3

Dilemma!

Resources

People puppets

What you do

Introduce some people puppets into your setting. Give them a name, age and personal history. Involve these characters in the daily life of the setting over a period of time. Involve them in group tasks, use them for question and answer sessions, sit them in the book corner to share stories and include them in games and activities.

Once the characters are well established and the children are independently including them in their play, use them to present dilemmas and raise issues that prompt debate and discussion about right and wrong. For example:

[Puppet] is worried because he broke the next door neighbour's window with a ball. No-one knows it was him and he doesn't want to be found out.
[Puppet's] friend took some sweets from the corner shop without paying and told [Puppet] not to tell anyone.
[Puppet] wants to share a secret with the children. Her mum and dad don't know that she only pretends to put her seatbelt on when she is in the car.
[Puppet] was at a birthday party on the weekend and when she got home she realised her pockets were full of toy food from her friend's play kitchen.
When [Puppet] got told off by his dad yesterday evening he decided to leave the house and walk round to grandma's on his own without telling anyone.
[Puppet] argues with his mum about brushing his teeth every morning. [Puppet] likes to brush them after breakfast but mum likes him to do it as soon as he gets up.

For each problem, ask the children to comfort and advise their puppet friend. Ask them to explain what they think about the puppet's behaviour and why. Do they think the puppet has done anything wrong? What would be the right thing to do? What do they think could happen as a result? How can the puppet solve the problem and make things better?

How does this promote the rule of law?

Young children relate really well to people puppets and readily accept them as members of the group. The puppets are great for presenting problems and fostering discussion about

important issues. In this case puppets are used to get children considering the difference between right and wrong and thinking about the possible consequences and repercussions of behaving in particular ways.

Key questions

- How would you feel if that happened to you?
- Do you think it is right to behave that way?
- Why was it wrong to behave that way?
- What might happen if you…?
- Why do you think that happened?
- What would you do if…?
- What do you think [puppet] should do?
- Who do you think is right/wrong? Why?

Curriculum links

PSED: Confident to speak to others about own needs, wants, interests and opinions; talks about own and others' behaviour, and its consequences, and knows that some behaviour is unacceptable.
CL: Listens and responds to ideas expressed by others in conversation or discussion; uses talk to organise, sequence and clarify thinking, ideas, feelings and events.

Activity 4

Beanbag catch

Resources

10 red and 10 green beanbags
7 red and 7 green hula hoops
7 red and 7 green sashes or T-shirts

What you do

Play this game with a maximum of 14 children divided into two teams of seven.

Allocate a colour (red or green, for example) to each team and give the children corresponding coloured sashes or T-shirts to wear. Give five children from each team a hula hoop that matches their team colour.

Place a red and green hula hoop side by side at either end of a large open space. Then drop 10 matching coloured beanbags in each hoop at one end of the space.

Help the children with hoops spread themselves evenly across the middle of the space. Ask the two children from each team without a hoop to go and stand next to the hoops at either end of the space.

Each team needs to get all 10 of their beanbags from one end of the space to the other. They need to do this by passing the beanbags from one teammate to the next without anyone from the other team intercepting them. The children standing next to the hoops filled with beanbags must take one beanbag at a time and throw it to the nearest person in their team. This person must then throw the beanbag to another person in their team and so on until the beanbag reaches the child standing next to the hoop at the other end of the space. Children are not allowed to leave their hoops. They are allowed to set one foot outside the hoop but the other must always remain inside. If a child from the other team catches the beanbag, they can then try and get that beanbag across the space to their hoop (intercepting and stealing it). If a beanbag lands on the floor out of reach, it is out of play and cannot be retrieved. The team that safely transports all (or the most) beanbags across first is the winner.

How does this promote the rule of law?

Following the rule of law involves paying attention, listening, processing, understanding and following instructions. Playing games like this also demonstrates the importance of rules for ensuring fair play, order and safety.

Key questions

- Do you understand the rules?
- Can you tell me what you have to do?
- Are you playing fair?
- What would happen if everyone ignored the rules?
- Do you think that is fair?
- How does it make you feel when someone from the other team breaks the rules?
- Is it safe to play like that?

Curriculum links

PSED: Talks about own and others' behaviour and its consequences, and knows that some behaviour is unacceptable; works as part of a group or class, and understands and follows the rules.
CL: Listens attentively in a range of situations; follows instructions involving several ideas.
PD: Shows increasing control over an object in throwing and catching it.

Individual liberty

Activity 1

We've all got talent!

Resources

Raised platform to use as a stage
Playground chalks
Costumes
Musical instruments
Microphones
CD/MP3 player and a selection of CDs
Puppet theatre and puppets
Storybooks

What you do

Set up a stage indoors or outside using crates or large hollow blocks. Otherwise mark out a stage area using playground chalks. Set out rows of small chairs for the audience. If the stage is outdoors put a battery powered CD/MP3 player nearby with a selection of music to choose from. Provide costumes and musical instruments.

Explain you are going to host an impromptu talent show. Allow the children the freedom to use the stage in whichever way they choose. They might dress up and get up to sing and dance, they may just use the opportunity for show and tell. Some children may prefer to use a puppet theatre. If the children are stuck for ideas, provide inspiration with popular well-known storybooks that the children can retell from memory.

Encourage reluctant performers to participate in other ways. They might like to create some background scenery for the stage. They could operate the music station or play musical instruments from the side. The aim of the activity is to help children grow in confidence so allow them to participate at their own comfort level.

Use the stage for story time. Ask the children to be the audience and get up there to perform an oral telling of a traditional tale. Invite willing volunteers to come up onto the stage and join in with repeated refrains and character parts.

How does this promote individual liberty?

If someone has self-confidence and good communication skills they will be more able to enjoy their right to individual liberty. Encouraging children to perform in front of each other in a safe space helps them to develop this confidence and enables them to practise their speaking and listening skills. Children on stage learn how to make themselves heard while those off stage practise how to listen and attend. Meanwhile, those who are

less confident performing can still participate and practise these same skills in alternative supporting roles.

Key questions

- How can you make sure everyone can hear you clearly?
- What did you like about their performance?
- Would you like to join in?
- Is there anything you can do to help?
- What is your talent?
- Is there another way you could take part?
- What would you like to show everyone?
- What makes a good audience?

Curriculum links

PSED: Can describe self in positive terms and talk about abilities; confident to speak in a familiar group, will talk about their ideas, and will choose the resources they need for the chosen activities.
CL: Listens attentively in a range of situations; expresses themselves effectively, showing awareness of listeners' needs.
EAD: Represents their own ideas, thoughts and feelings through design and technology, art, music, dance, role play and stories.

Activity 2

A problem shared

Resources

None needed for this activity

What you do

Look for problems in the setting that directly affect the children and ask for their help in finding solutions. Bring the children together and present them with problems as they occur.
For example:

- The paintbrushes have gone hard. They can no longer be used and have to be thrown away.

- Jessica just slipped on the floor in the wet area and banged her head.

- When watering the plants on the windowsill the pictures on the wall below got wet and were ruined.

- The small balls keep flying over the fence into the playground.

- There are not enough small cars for everyone to have one each.

- There are no more grapes left and some children have not yet had their snack.

- Some children are not getting a turn with the computers and tablets.

- There is soft cheese spread all over the wooden blocks.

Ask the children if they can explain how the problem might have occurred (but take care to avoid apportioning blame to individuals). Once they have come to a conclusion ask them to think about how they can solve the problem. Finally, ask them to think about how such a problem might be avoided in the future.

How does this promote individual liberty?

Individual liberty includes the right to free speech. This right can only be enjoyed if people are able to listen to each other; to understand, accept and evaluate others' ideas, views and opinions. Presenting children with problems and asking them to discuss possible solutions gives them a chance to learn how to express themselves as well as listen to others.

Key questions

- Why do you think that happened?
- How do you think we can prevent that from happening again?
- What should we do next time?
- What can we do about this?
- How can we make sure everyone has a turn?
- Do you think that is a fair solution?
- How would that work?
- Do you agree? Why/why not?

Curriculum links

PSED: Takes account of one another's ideas about how to organise their activity; confident to speak in a familiar group, will talk about their ideas, and will choose the resources they need; talks about own and others' behaviour and its consequences.
CL: Gives their attention to what others say and responds appropriately; listens and responds to ideas expressed by others in conversation or discussion; uses talk to organise, sequence and clarify thinking, ideas, feelings and events; develops their own explanations by connecting ideas or events.
UW: Talks about why things happen and how things work.

Individual liberty

Activity 3   Provoking a reaction

What you do

I have written in the past about how to set up provocations that aim to spark the children's interests and foster creative thinking (see resources). A provocation is something that evokes a creative response. It might be an object, event, place, photo, story, piece of music or picture, for example, that stirs the children's curiosity and inspires them to create their own artworks, stories and play narratives in response. Often a provocation will be set up by an adult in relation to an observed interest amongst the children. An alternative approach is to turn the tables and invite the children to come up with provocations of their own.

Give the children (and their parents) plenty of notice by writing home at the beginning of term and explaining you would like them to look for something strange and unusual to bring into the setting sometime in the next six weeks. Explain it can be an object, artwork or photograph of something and add that it should be something the children can touch and examine closely.

As and when the children bring in their unusual items, put them on display where the children can get their hands on them and have a good close look. Ask the children who brought in each item to explain where they got it from/where they saw it and if they know what it is/anything about it. Provide magnifying glasses, digital cameras, clipboards, pencils, and art and craft materials to enable the children to respond in any way they choose. If possible, allow them to incorporate the items into their play. If the children fail to bring something in, you can always bring something in yourself or create your own provocations (see photo above).

How does this promote Individual liberty?

Provocations encourage children to exercise their right to individual liberty because they elicit individual creative thought and expression and encourage them to talk together, as they tell each other their ideas and opinions.

Key questions/prompts

- Wow! Look at this!
- Where do you think s/he got it from?
- Have you seen anything like that before?
- Tell me about what you are doing.
- That looks interesting.
- What made you think of that?

Curriculum links

PSED: Explains own knowledge and understanding, and asks appropriate questions of others; confident to speak to others about own interests and opinions.
CL: Gives their attention to what others say and responds appropriately; uses talk to organise, sequence and clarify thinking and ideas.
UW: Notices detailed features of objects in their environment; looks closely at similarities, differences, patterns and change.
EAD: Uses what they have learnt about media and materials in original ways, thinking about uses and purposes; represents their own ideas, thoughts and feelings through design and technology, art, music, dance, role play and stories.

Activity 4

Natural creations

Resources

Natural woodland setting
Clay

What you do

Take the children to a natural setting where they have access to an abundance of natural materials. Tell them they can work alone, in pairs or in groups to create a piece of wild art. It can be a sculpture, picture or installation (a working creation that fits into but alters the natural setting – see the picture of a 'bridge' on the right).

Bring out some clay. Explain it is a natural material that comes from the ground and the children are allowed to incorporate it into their artworks if they would like to. Clay is a great addition to wild art because it can be used as a base into which objects like cones, flowers and leaves can be pressed, but also to stick things together and secure objects in place.

As the children set to work ask them to explain what they are doing. What are they creating and why? When everyone has finished walk around in small groups to look at the different artworks. Encourage the children to talk about what they have created and how, and invite others to ask questions. Photograph the artworks to display back at the setting.

This activity is also possible in a beach setting, where the children have access to shells, seaweed and pebbles, and have the option of sculpting the sand.

How does this promote individual liberty?

Part of individual liberty is freedom of expression. Children should be encouraged to express themselves and communicate their ideas, thoughts and feelings in all kinds of ways. Activities like this open up opportunities for children to create something different from the usual paintings, drawings and models they would produce with conventional art materials.

Key questions/prompts

- This looks interesting.
- What are you going to use that for?
- What else do you think you could use?
- Why did you choose to use that?

- How are you going to join that together?
- What material would work best?
- Tell me about what you have made.

Curriculum links

PSED: Takes account of one another's ideas about how to organise their activity; confident to speak in a familiar group, will talk about their ideas, and will choose the resources they need for their chosen activities.
CL: Gives their attention to what others say and responds appropriately, while engaged in another activity; uses talk to organise, sequence and clarify thinking and ideas.
PD: Handles tools, objects, construction and malleable materials safely and with increasing control.
UW: Can talk about some of the things they have observed such as plants, natural and found objects; talks about features of their own immediate environment.
EAD: Manipulates materials to achieve a planned effect; constructs with a purpose in mind, using a variety of resources; selects appropriate resources and adapts work where necessary; selects tools and techniques needed to shape, assemble and join materials they are using.

Mutual respect and tolerance

Activity 1

Story wall

Resources

Display board
Shoe boxes
Craft materials
Staple gun
Long pins
A selection of stories for children from different religions (see resources)

What you do

Focus on one religion every couple of weeks. Use simple information books to find out about each religion and its associated festival celebrations and traditions. Use traditional stories to help the children better relate to and connect with each set of religious/cultural beliefs.

Work with small groups to create story dioramas in shoe boxes. Decorate the base and sides of the box to create a background to the scene and use craft materials to make characters and props to stand inside. Then ask the children to retell the story in their own words while you transcribe. More able children might like to write a sentence about the scene they have created/cultural themselves.

Create a world religion story wall. Use a staple gun or long pins to attach the shoe boxes to a display board along with the children's sentences and story retellings. Add more stories to the wall as the weeks go on.

How does this promote mutual respect and tolerance?

Stories are an age-appropriate way to help young children relate to the beliefs of others. In the UK we predominantly celebrate Christian festivals in many schools and most young children are familiar with the Christmas and Easter stories by the time they reach the end of Key Stage 1. It is important to balance this out by introducing children to a wider range of religious stories so they understand that British society is composed of people with many different beliefs and faiths.

Key questions

- What was the story about?

- Who were the main characters?
- Did we learn anything from the story?
- Which part of the story do you want to tell in your story box scene?
- Which culture/religion is this story from?
- Why is this story important?

Curriculum links

CL: Listens to stories, accurately anticipating key events and responds to what they hear with relevant comments; uses talk to organise, sequence and clarify thinking and ideas.
PD: Handles tools, objects, construction and malleable materials safely and with increasing control.
L: Writes simple sentences which can be read by themselves and others.
UW: Knows about similarities and differences between themselves and others, and among families, communities and traditions.
EAD: Constructs with a purpose in mind, using a variety of resources; uses simple tools and techniques competently and appropriately; selects tools and techniques need to shape, assemble and join materials they are using.

Activity 2

Symbolic art

Resources

Large laminated pictures of different religious symbols
Sheets of symbols printed in various shapes, colours
and sizes
Scissors
Pencil crayons and felt pens
Glue

What you do

Introduce a range of religious symbols to the children. Explain
that each religion has different symbols that represent the
various beliefs. For example:

- Christianity: Cross
- Islam: Crescent moon and star
- Judaism: Star of David
- Hinduism: Sanskrit Aum
- Buddhism: Dharma wheel
- Sikhism: Khanda

Tell the children that the many millions of people living in Britain
have different beliefs. Some people have no religion at all,
but many have a faith, follow a religion and worship a god(s).
Everyone has the right and freedom to choose their faith and
follow whichever religion they wish. We all exist together in a
multifaith and multicultural society.

Ask the children to use the pictures of religious symbols to
create collages that represent multifaith Britain and the many
millions of British people with different faiths and beliefs who
live alongside each other. The children can use the symbols
to create any design of pattern or picture they choose. Mount
the children's pictures on a wall display featuring short, simple
explanations of what each symbol represents.

You could also cut out a shape of the United Kingdom from
a large piece of card and invite each child to stick on a small
paper symbol that represents their own religion. Ask adults to
add theirs too. For those who do not have a religion create a
symbol, a sunshine, for instance.

How does this promote mutual respect and tolerance?

This is a simple visual way of demonstrating that British society is
comprised of many different faiths and beliefs. This is especially

helpful for children who live in tight-knit single faith communities
with little exposure to people from different cultural backgrounds.

Key questions

- Have you seen this symbol before?
- Do you know which religion this symbol represents?
- Do you know what this symbol means?
- Do you and your family follow a religion?
- Does your family go to church/temple/synagogue?

Curriculum links

PSED: Shows sensitivity to others' feelings, and forms
positive relationships with adults and other children; will
communicate freely about own home and community.
PD: Handles tools safely and with increasing control.
UW: Knows about similarities and differences between
themselves and others, and among families, communities
and traditions.
EAD: Uses simple tools and techniques competently and
appropriately.

Mutual respect and tolerance

Activity 3

Same difference

What you do

Broaden the children's awareness and understanding of different faiths by taking them to visit various places of worship in and around the local community. Invite local religious leaders into the setting to meet the children and ask them if they would mind taking you on a tour of their particular place of worship.

Before each visit find out about any rules and/or restrictions that you and the children need to adhere to. For instance: Will the children be required to remove shoes? If so, will bare feet be allowed or will they need socks? Are there any rules about clothing? Are there any restrictions on where men and women are allowed to go? Is there anything sacred that the children must not touch?

During each visit ask your guide to point out important symbols, objects, statues and artefacts and to explain their significance. Ask them to show you a copy of the religious text they use, what the script is called and if there are any special rules about how the book is stored, handled and read. Ask about worship and prayer; how often do people come? Is there a particular holy day? Is there a special way to pray?

Once the children have visited a selection of places bring them together to create a large display about the different religions they have been introduced to. Compare and contrast the symbolic dress of each religious leader, the architecture of each place of worship, the different holy texts and the many symbols, objects and artefacts of religious significance. Use all of this to help the children understand that different religions share many similarities in the lessons they teach.

How does this promote mutual respect and tolerance?

Meeting religious leaders and visiting places of worship is a particularly powerful way of breaking down barriers. Intolerance and fear come from ignorance and misunderstanding. Meeting people of different faiths and religions, entering their space and finding out about their beliefs is an important experience for young children, removing the mystery and demonstrating that underneath the surface people are fundamentally the same.

Key questions

- Have you seen anything like this before?
- Do you and your family go somewhere to worship?
- Do you read/hear stories from a holy book?
- Do you know any prayers?
- How often do you go there?
- Can you remember what this was called?
- Do you remember if there were any special rules?

Curriculum links

PSED: Shows sensitivity to others' feelings, and forms positive relationships with adults and other children; communicates freely about own home and community; aware of boundaries set, and of behavioural expectations.
CL: Listens attentively in a range of situations; begins to understand 'why' and 'how' questions; uses talk to organise, sequence and clarify thinking, ideas, feelings and events.
UW: Knows about similarities and differences between themselves and others, and among families, communities and traditions.

Activity 4

Flying visit

Resources

Old patterned rug
Artefacts, foods, music and clothing from different cultures
Pictures of places around the world
Craft materials

What you do

- One evening transform the setting so when the children enter the next day it looks like they have arrived in a different country.
- Rearrange the furniture to create the impression of a market square or street.
- Set up role play market stalls selling clothing and food from your chosen place.
- Set up a role play café with real foods from this place.
- Download some street sounds from this place from the Internet and play them in the background.
- Have some traditional music playing in the café.
- Dress up in the clothing worn by people local to the area.
- Provide role play clothing for the children to wear.
- Display vocabulary from the country's language and mount recordable buttons (see resources) with key words for the children to listen to.
- Set up craft activities related to your place of choice.
- Print off and display pictures from your chosen country all around the setting. For example, eateries, market places, streets, buildings, animals and geographical surroundings.

Lay out an old rug outside of where you have set up the scene, in a corridor, hallway or outdoor area, for example. When the children arrive in the morning take them straight to the rug for registration and explain you are going to fly on a magic carpet to another country for the day. Then count down and take off, pretending to fly for a few minutes before standing up and walking into the setting.

Let the children explore the role play settings, try on the clothes, taste the food and do traditional crafts. Learn some key vocabulary and traditional dances and songs. Look at a map to find where the country is and see how far you have travelled. Round off the day with a traditional story from the country you have visited, then get back on the magic carpet to fly back to Britain.

How does this promote mutual respect and tolerance?

Promoting British values involves introducing children to a variety of cultures and helping them to understand how different people

live. Young children learn best through first-hand experience and although it is not possible to literally take them on a trip around the world, with a little imagination you can bring the sights, sounds, smells and tastes of different countries and cultures to them.

Key questions

- Where do you think we are?
- Do you know anyone who comes from this country?
- What does that smell/taste like?
- Would you like to try...?
- Have you ever seen anything like that before?
- Where would you like to go next time?

Curriculum links

PSED: Confident to try new activities, and say why they like some activities more than others.
UW: Knows about similarities and differences between themselves and others, and among families, communities and traditions.
EAD: Captures experiences and responses with a range of media, such as music, dance and paint and other materials or words.

Collecting evidence

The recent introduction of the new Common Inspection Framework means that early years providers are now required to provide evidence that they are actively promoting British values within their settings. As demonstrated in the introduction, British values are already implicit within the themes and principles of the EYFS. **This means there should be no need to go out of the way to collect additional evidence specifically related to promoting the values.**

The Revised Prevent Duty Guidance for England and Wales reiterates the legal responsibility of schools and nurseries under the Education Act 2002 to deliver a 'broad and balanced curriculum which promotes the spiritual, moral, cultural, mental and physical development of pupils and prepares them for the opportunities, responsibilities and experiences of later life'. The Statutory Framework for the EYFS identifies seven 'important and inter-connected' areas of learning and development and sets out the expectation that children should experience an educational programme that involves 'activities and experiences' across all seven. Furthermore, when planning these activities and experiences, practitioners must take into account the three characteristics of effective learning: playing and exploring, active learning, and creating and thinking critically. **If you can demonstrate the children in your setting are experiencing a broad and balanced educational programme that ignites their individual interests, enables them to participate to the best of their ability, encourages independence and creativity, and broadens their knowledge and understanding of the world, you are actively promoting British values.**

In addition, the Prevent duty guidance also refers to the Education and Inspections Act 2006, which highlights the duty of the school inspectorate to report upon 'the contribution made by the school to community cohesion'. This is supported by the Statutory Framework for the EYFS, which 'seeks to provide… equality of opportunity and anti-discriminatory practice, ensuring that every child is included and supported'. The underlying principle of a unique child is that all children and their families are valued and respected equally and not discriminated against on any basis. Furthermore, it is expected that practitioners provide an enabling environment where diversity is valued in terms of the richness it brings to the setting. **If you can demonstrate that the practitioners in your setting have inclusive, respectful and tolerant attitudes towards all children and their families, and the activities you plan and the fabric of your setting reflect the diversity of its intake, you are actively promoting British values.**

An outstanding setting will be able to demonstrate that British values are embedded within its culture through everyday practice. This means:

- Practitioners will listen to children and engage them in dialogue.
- Children will be confident and willing to speak out and voice their opinions.
- Children will play collaboratively or alongside others and demonstrate inclusive behaviour and attitudes.
- Children will experience a broad and balanced educational programme.
- The educational programme that includes activities that broaden children's knowledge and understanding of the world by introducing them to cultures and communities beyond their immediate experience.
- Children will be involved in planning.
- The setting will recognise the prime importance of personal, social and emotional development in its planning.
- Observation records will include space for assessment notes and next steps.
- Practitioners will share observations with children and invite them to self-assess.
- Observation and assessment records will include notes from parents and children.
- Learning displays, resources, equipment and images will reflect a diversity of cultures and ethnicities.
- Information displays, visual materials and labelling will be translated into relevant languages.
- All children will be treated fairly and equally.
- Practitioners will demonstrate a positive attitude towards different cultures, faiths and beliefs.
- Practitioners will challenge gender, cultural and racial stereotyping.
- The setting will work to forge positive relationships with parents, including ensuring all parents have access to the information and support they need.
- The setting will have up-to-date policies related to equality, diversity and inclusion, and English as an additional language.

All of these things are requirements of the EYFS anyway. You will already be doing them. All you have to do is evidence your good practice. The attitudes and behaviour of your staff and children will exemplify how well embedded British values are in your setting. The displays and learning environment will provide further evidence, as will your policy and procedure documents (find further guidance on this in the companion to this book *Promoting Fundamental British Values in the Early Years*).

You can also provide evidence in your observation and assessment documentation. The observation document opposite includes prompts to help you highlight which EYFS areas of learning and development the children are encountering. It also provides space for making assessment notes and considering next steps.

Observation record

Child's name		
Observer's name		
Area of provision/Focused activity		
Date	**Start time:**	
	End time:	

Observation notes
This should be a factual report of what the child(ren) did and said without personal comment, opinion or judgement.

Area of learning and development	PSED	CL	PD	M	L	UW	EAD

Assessment Notes
Refer to the overview of the four British values on page 4 and consider how the activity or play is promoting these values. Is the activity or play fostering any particular skills, aptitudes, abilities or attitudes that underpin any of the four values? Do the children need more guidance in any of these areas? Is there an area of your provision that could be altered or enhanced so that it better promotes such values?

Implications for future planning
Demonstrate here that you are using observations to inform planning. Refer to the planning matrix on page 5. Is there an activity from this book that you could use to help the children develop their knowledge, skills and understanding further?

Comments from parents/children
Demonstrate here that parents and children are actively involved in documenting, assessing and planning learning.

Resources and Further Reading

Resources

Democracy
- *The Election* by Eleanor Levenson and Marek Jagucki (Fisherton Press)
- *Never Too Young: How Young Children Can Take Responsibility and Make Decisions* by Judy Miller (Save the Children)
- *Starting With Choice: Inclusive Strategies for Consulting Young Children* by Mary Dickins, Sue Emerson and Pat Gordon-Smith (Save the Children)
- *Making Waves: Exciting parachute games to develop self-confidence and team-building skills* by Jenny Mosely and Helen Sonnet (LDA)
- Giant Jumbo Elephant and Giant Dog puzzles (www.knottoys.com)
- Indoor Puzzle Play House (www.softfloorkids.co.uk)

Rule of law
- *Watch Out! On the Road* by Claire Llewellyn and Mike Gordon (Barron's Educational)
- *Golden Rules Animal Stories* by Donna Luck and Juliet Doyle (Positive Press)
- *Know and Follow Rules* and *Understand and Care* by Cheri J Meiners (Free Spirit Publishing)
- *50 Fantastic Ideas for Exploring Emotions* by Sally and Phill Featherstone (Featherstone Education)
- Role play road safety set (www.tts-group.co.uk)
- BIG traffic lights (www.adventuretoys.co.uk)
- People puppets (www.puppetsbypost.com)

Individual liberty
- *We Are All Born Free* by Amnesty International (Frances Lincoln Children's Books)
- *My World, Your World* by Melanie Walsh (Corgi Children's)
- *My Little Book of Big Freedoms* by Chris Riddell (Amnesty International UK)
- *50 Fantastic Ideas for Imaginative Thinking* by Marianne Sargent (Featherstone Education)
- *The Project Approach in Early Years Provision* by Marianne Sargent (Practical Pre-School Books)

Mutual respect and tolerance
- *Whoever You Are* by Mem Fox and Leslie Staub (Harcourt Children's Books)
- White Wolves Stories from World Religions series from A&C Black: *Rama and Sita* (Hinduism), *Noah's Ark* (Christianity), *The Golem* (Judaism), *The Guru and the King* (Sikhism), *The Dinner of Smells* (Islam), *Siddhartha and the Swan* (Buddhism)
- Festival Time series from Frances Lincoln Children's Books: *Lighting a Lamp: A Divali Story*, *Eight Candles to Light: A Chanukah Story*, *Sweet Dates to Eat: A Ramadan and Eid Story*

- Holidays and Festivals series from Heinemann Library: *Hanukkah*, *Diwali*, *Christmas*, *Ramadan* and *Id-ul-Fitr*
- For information about a range of world religions with links to examples of holy texts go to: www.bbc.co.uk/religion/religions/
- Multicultural Resources for Early Years Education (www.little-linguist.co.uk/multicultural-resources-for-children.html)
- Festival Enhancements for 3-7yrs (http://earlyexcellence.com/product-category/indoor-enhancements-3-7-years/festival-enhancements-3-7yrs/)
- Talking-Point Recordable Buttons (www.tts-group.com)

Further reading

- *Common Inspection Framework: Education, Skills and Early Years* by Ofsted (The Stationary Office)
- *Common Inspection Framework, British Values and You* by the Professional Association for Childcare and Early Years (PACEY)
- *Critical Skills in the Early Years* by Vicki Charlesworth (Network Continuum Education)
- *Prevent Strategy* by HM Government (The Stationary Office)
- *Promoting Fundamental British Values in the Early Years* by Marianne Sargent (Practical Pre-School Books)
- *Revised Prevent Duty Guidance for England and Wales* by HM Government (The Stationary Office)